The BIG BOOK OF GROSS JOKES

• • • • •

by Julius Alvin

Kensington Books
http://www.kensingtonbooks.com

KENSINGTON BOOKS are published by

Kensington Publishing Corp.
850 Third Avenue
New York, NY 10022

ISBN 1-57566-235-3

First Kensington Trade Paperback Printing: December, 1997
10 9 8 7 6 5 4 3 2 1

Printed in the United States of America

To Paul Dinas at Kensington Publishing, who let me tell him most of the jokes contained in these pages and was a terrific audience;

To the loving memory of my father, who loved a great dirty joke more than anyone;

To my mother, who never understood them;

To an immigrant Lebanese cab driver named Jameel Amir Pishtipple, who once asked me, in all seriousness, the words one only dreams of someday hearing: "How do you get to Carnegie Hall?"

To my friend Michael Siskind, who ripped off a huge fart during the principal's assembly speech in the gymnasium of Chestnut Street Elementary, where two hundred kids were in attendance. Mike not only got the biggest laugh I've ever heard to this day, he also taught me the one essential rule of comedy: Timing is everything.

To my friend Bradley Levine, who burp-talked his entire Bar Mitzvah to the horror of a hundred friends and relatives. Brad taught me another essential rule of comedy: Fuck 'em if they can't take a joke;

And to every peckerhead who ever forgot or messed up a punchline, whip it together or don't waste our time.

"I need this book like I need a hole in the head!"
—Ex-President John F. Kennedy

IN A WORD, SEX *1*

GROSS GAY AND LESBIAN JOKES *29*

GROSS ETHNIC JOKES *57*

GROSS CELEBRITY JOKES *93*

SO GROSS EVEN WE WERE OFFENDED *117*

TRULY SICK JOKES *147*

NOW THAT'S REALLY SICK! *167*

IN
A
WORD,
SEX

• • • • • • •

On the night of her wedding, the young bride pulled her mother aside and said, "Mama, tell me how to make my new husband happy."

Her mother replied, "Well, when two people love each other, they make love."

"Oh, I know all about fucking, Mama," the bride responded. "I want to know how to make lasagna."

• • •

Two perverts were watching a film in a dark movie theater. When Demi Moore appeared on the screen, the first pervert said to the other, "I've had her, you know."

A few minutes later, Julia Roberts appeared on the screen. The first pervert said to the second pervert, "You know, I've had her, too."

Later, Melanie Griffith appeared on the screen. The second pervert said to his friend, "I suppose you had her, too?"

"Shhh," the first pervert replied. "I'm having her now."

• • •

So this man is having a vasectomy. During the delicate operation, one of his testicles falls onto the floor, and before the nurse can pick it up, the doctor steps on it.

The doctor tells the nurse, "Don't worry, we can replace it. Get me a very small onion." She does, and the doctor replaces the missing ball with the onion.

A few weeks later, the patient stops by to see the doctor, who asks him what seems to be the problem.

"Well, it's like this," the patient replies. "Every time I take a piss, my eyes water. Every time I come, I get heartburn. And every time I pass a Burger King, I get a hard-on!"

• • •

Why do women in Canada use hockey pucks instead of tampons?

They last two periods.

• • •

What do you get when you cross a prostitute and a pit bull?

The last blow job you'll ever get.

• • •

What's the difference between a penis and a pay-check?

You don't have to beg your wife to blow your pay-check.

• • •

So the guy walks into a singles bar and picks out the prettiest girl he can find. Sitting down next to her, he reaches into his pocket and pulls out a box. Inside the box is a small frog.

"He's really cute," the blonde says. "Does he do tricks?"

"He sure does," the guy says. "He eats pussy."

The blonde is skeptical, so the guy convinces her to return to his apartment to prove to her that his pet frog does, indeed, eat pussy. The blonde gets undressed and gets on the bed, spreading her legs. The guy puts the frog down between her legs, but the frog doesn't budge. The blonde says, "Well?"

"Okay, moron," the guy says to the frog. "I'm only going to show you one more time."

• • •

Norman walked into the neighborhood saloon and announced that he was divorcing his wife. The bartender asked why.

"Well," Norman said, "yesterday was her birthday, so I took her to the fanciest restaurant in town."

"So?" the bartender asked.

"So I ordered a bottle of their best champagne, and I made her a toast—'To the best woman a man could have.'"

"What's wrong with that?"

"Three of the waiters joined in."

• • •

"My wife would make a great soccer goalie," one man said to his friend. "I haven't scored in months."

• • •

"I knew the honeymoon was over," the same man said to his friend, "when I started going out every Thursday night with the boys."

"What's wrong with that?"

"So did she."

• • •

Hear about the woman who worked at a sperm bank and got pregnant?

She was arrested for embezzlement.

• • •

What's hairy and sucks blood?

Cunt Dracula.

• • •

"I'm sorry to say," the doctor said to the man, "that after examining your wife, we've discovered that she has acute angina."

"I know," her husband said, "but what's wrong with her?"

• • •

What do you call an anorexic with a yeast infection?

A quarter-pounder with cheese.

• • •

So the doctor says to Ed, "You have a rare disease. The only thing that can cure you is fresh breast milk."

Ed advertises for a wet nurse. A beautiful woman responds to his ad and agrees to wet-nurse him. Their first time, Ed is happily sucking away and is pretty good at it, so much so that the wet nurse finds herself becoming aroused.

Feeling Ed sucking her tit, she moans, "Is there anything else I can do for you?"

"You wouldn't have any chocolate chip cookies, would you?" Ed asks.

• • •

Question: If girls are made of sugar and spice, why do they taste like anchovies?

• • •

So Bill's wife was in a terrible car accident and is in intensive care. Bill rushes to the hospital, where the doctor tells him, "Research shows that oral sex speeds a patient's recovery. I suggest you try it. I'll instruct the nurses to leave you both alone for the next hour."

Five minutes later, buzzers and bells bring doctors and nurses to the room. The doctors work furiously to save Bill's wife. When she is stabilized, the doctor asks him, "What went wrong?"

"I don't know," Bill replies. "I think she choked."

• • •

The city slicker was puzzled when he saw the farmer plowing his fields with a bull. He asked the farmer, "Don't you have a horse or a tractor?"

"Got both," the farmer replied.

"Then why are you plowing your fields with a bull?"

"I'm trying to teach him that he ain't here just for romance."

• • •

What do you call oral sex with Yuppies?

Sixty-something.

• • •

A woman walks into her doctor's office for a physical. She takes off her clothes to show that on her chest is an outline of the letter *C.* "Excuse me," the doctor says. "But how the hell did that letter get on you?" The woman confesses that her husband went to Connecticut University and the night before fucked her when he was wearing his varsity sweater. The doctor finishes her physical and calls in his next patient. Sure enough, she has a large *T* covering her tits. She explains that her husband went to Texas University and the night before fucked her when he was wearing his varsity sweater. The doctor completes her physical and calls in his next patient—a woman with an *M* covering her chest. "Don't tell me," the doctor says, "he went to Michigan." "Nope," the woman says, "she went to Wisconsin."

• • •

A woman hails a cab in Manhattan in the middle of rush hour. She gives the cabbie her destination, which is forty blocks uptown. When they get there, the cabby turns to her and says, "That'll be six bucks, lady."

The woman smiles and tells him, "I'm afraid I don't have any money." She proceeds to pull her dress up and flash her snatch at him. "Maybe this will do?"

The cabby looks down at her pussy and says, "Lady, ain't you got anything smaller?"

• • •

On the occasion of their tenth anniversary, a man sends his wife a dozen roses. When the delivery boy comes to the house, the wife says to him, "Flowers, just great. This means my husband will expect me to spend the next two days with my legs up in the air."

The delivery boy responded, "You may want to try using a vase first, ma'am."

• • •

A man goes into a bar and orders a shot of whiskey. He downs it in one gulp, then orders another, which he also downs in one gulp.

This goes on for some time, until the man has ten empty shot glasses in front of him.

"So what are you celebrating?" the bartender asks.

"I'm celebrating my first blow job," the man says.

"Congratulations," the bartender replies, and starts to pour him another. "Have one on the house."

"No thanks," the man says. "If ten didn't get the taste out of my mouth, eleven sure won't."

• • •

A guy takes his parrot to a veterinarian. He says, "Doc, I know this will be hard to believe, but I think my parrot is horny."

"Horny?" asks the vet. "How can you tell?"

"I wanna get laid, I wanna get laid," the parrot starts squawking.

The vet says, "I guess he is horny. For fifty bucks, I have a female parrot. I'll put her in the cage with your bird."

The parrot says, "Pay him. Pay him."

The owner gives the vet fifty dollars.

The vet takes the female parrot and puts it inside the cage with the horny male parrot, then covers the cage.

Moments later, there is squawking and feathers are flying everywhere. The vet lifts the cover from the cage. Inside, the male parrot holds the female parrot down with one claw and is ripping out her feathers with the other.

The parrot is screeching, "For fifty bucks, I want you naked!"

• • •

What's the definition of a glass pussy?

A womb with a view.

• • •

One Sunday during Mass, Father O'Brien sees thirteen-year-old Tommy take fifteen dollars out of the collection plate. The priest says nothing, figuring that the kid needs it. The next Sunday during Mass, the father sees Tommy take fifteen more dollars out of the collection plate.

Father O'Brien decides to confront young Tommy. After Mass, he takes the boy aside and asks him, "Why do you keep stealing fifteen dollars from the collection plate?"

"To tell the truth, Father," Tommy says. "I needed the money for a blow job."

Father O'Brien has never heard this expression before and isn't sure what it means. He sends Tommy away and later runs across Sister Mary.

He asks the nun, "Sister, what's a blow job?"

Sister Mary says, "Oh, about fifteen dollars."

• • •

A couple had been married five years and their sex life was getting a bit dull. One night, the husband came home and announced to his wife, "Honey, tonight we're going to make love a different way. Tonight we're going to make love lying back to back."

"What fun is that?" the wife wants to know.

"Plenty," the husband says. "I invited another couple."

• • •

"My mother-in-law is impossible," one guy says to his friend. "She broke up my marriage."

"How did she do that?" his friend wants to know.

"My wife came home and found us in bed together."

• • •

Two Hollywood agents are walking on Ventura Boulevard when they pass a beautiful blonde.

One says to the other, "Boy, would I like to screw her."

The other agent replies, "Out of what?"

• • •

What did the butcher do when he saw his store on fire?

He grabbed his meat and beat it.

• • •

Why did the condom fly across the room?

It got pissed off.

• • •

What do blondes say during sex?

"You guys all on the same team?"

• • •

What's the difference between a blimp and three hundred and sixty-five blow jobs?

One's a Goodyear, the other's a great year.

• • •

Why do blondes wear underwear?

To keep their ankles warm.

• • •

Why are blondes so quiet when they fuck?

They don't talk to strangers.

• • •

Did you hear about the Biblical whore?

She was picked up for trying to make a prophet in the temple.

• • •

What's the toughest thing about acting in a porno movie?

Learning your loins.

• • •

Then there was the eighty-five-year-old man who was charged with rape. His lawyer asked, "So did you do it?"

"No," the old man said. "But I was so flattered, I pleaded guilty."

• • •

What did the stockbroker's wife tell her husband when she cheated on him?

"Sorry, dear, but I've gone public."

• • •

Why is an ugly girl like a bedspread?

They both get turned down every night.

• • •

After a fight with Lois Lane, Superman is flying around, looking for action. He sees it: Lying naked, spread-eagled and sleeping on a Himalayan mountain is Wonder Woman. Superman flies down, takes out his cock, and fucks away. As he flies off, Wonder Woman wakes up and says, "Whoa—what happened?" The Invisible Man replies, "I don't know, but does my asshole hurt!"

• • •

A ninety-year-old woman in a nursing home decided that she still wanted to have sex. She ran into the recreation room, lifted her dress, and, showing her snatch, cried, "Super pussy! Super pussy!"

There were no takers. The old lady ran into another room, lifted her dress, and called out, "Super pussy! Super pussy!"

There were still no takers.

The old lady ran into the dining room, where one old man was sitting. She ran up to him and lifted her dress. "Super pussy, super pussy!" she cried.

The old man looked at her and said, "I'll have the soup."

• • •

Why is Santa Claus a pervert?

He likes to come down chimneys.

• • •

Why is the little red schoolhouse red?

If you had eight periods, you'd be red, too.

• • •

A couple goes to see a marriage counselor. He says, "What seems to be the problem?"

The husband says, "We fight all the time."

"What do you fight about?" the marriage counselor asks.

"Our sex life," the wife replies, pointing to her husband. "The son of a bitch wants one!"

• • •

What's the difference between love and lust?

Lust never costs more than two-hundred dollars.

• • •

What did the flasher say to his victim during a blizzard?

"It's too cold. Mind if I just describe myself?"

• • •

What's the definition of "68"?

You do me, and I'll owe you one.

• • •

How do you stop a dog from humping your leg?

Give him a blow job.

• • •

A guy comes home from work one day to find his girlfriend packing her bags.

"What are you doing, honey?" he says to her.

"Alvin, I'm leaving you," she tells him.

"But why?" he asks. "Everything was going so well."

The girlfriend replies, "I'm leaving you because you're a pedophile!"

"Pedophile?" Alvin snorts. "That's a pretty big word for a seven-year-old!"

• • •

Why aren't lawyers breast-fed as babies?

Because their own mothers don't trust them.

• • •

How do you drown a blonde?

Tell her not to swallow.

• • •

What do you call a hooker who services sadists?

Someone who's strapped for cash.

• • •

What do you call a doctor who treats only fat women's pussies?

A rhinocologist.

• • •

What do you call an all-nude soap opera?

Genital Hospital.

• • •

A ten-year-old boy is dragged into court on a paternity suit. He hires the best lawyer in town.

At the hearing, the lawyer asks the young boy to stand up and unzip his fly before the judge. The lawyer reaches inside the boy's pants and pulls out his tiny, limp dick.

"Your honor," the lawyer begins, wagging the kid's doodle, "take a good look at this small, undeveloped penis. Is it possible that he could father a child with this?"

The lawyer continues on, wagging the kid's dick, until the kid mutters to the lawyer, "You better quit shaking it real soon or we're gonna blow this case!"

• • •

What's the definition of a sadist?

A proctologist who keeps his thermometer in the freezer.

• • •

What's the definition of sex?

One of the most beautiful, natural, and wholesome things that money can buy.

• • •

What's the difference between men and women when it comes to sex?

Women need a reason to have sex, men only need a place.

• • •

What is "34 ½"?

"69" for midgets.

• • •

Little Red Riding Hood is prancing through the forest. The big bad wolf jumps out from behind a tree and cries, "I'm going to eat you!"

Little Red Riding Hood says, "Eat, eat, eat! Doesn't anyone fuck anymore?"

• • •

What do you call a magician who likes to squeeze tits?

David Coppa-feel.

• • •

What do you call a sex club in Disneyworld?

Pluto's Retreat.

• • •

What's the best thing about sex education?

The oral exams.

• • •

Why did the Jew buy an artificial vagina in a sex shop?

He heard there was no sales tax on food items.

• • •

What's the definition of artificial insemination?

A technical knock-up.

• • •

Why did the dwarf get kicked out of the nudist colony?

He kept getting in everyone's hair.

• • •

A fifteen-year-old girl asks her father, "Daddy, can I borrow the car?"

Her father replies, "Yes, but only if you give me a blow job."

The girl is repulsed, but she really wants to use the car. She agrees. Her father drops his pants and shoves his daughter's head down on his cock.

The girls starts sucking, then spits in disgust and cries, "Geez, Daddy, your cock tastes just like shit!"

"Oh, that's right," her father remembers. "Your brother asked to borrow the car an hour ago."

• • •

What did the elephant say to the guy with a ten-inch dick?

"Very nice, but can you eat peanuts with it?"

• • •

What's white and rains down from the heavens?

The coming of the Lord.

• • •

On their honeymoon, the couple made love. Afterward, the bride punched her husband in the nose.

"What's that for?" the husband asked.

His new wife said, "That's for being a lousy lover!"

With this, the husband punched his wifc in thc nose.

"What's that for?" she asked.

"For knowing the difference!" the husband said.

• • •

What do peacocks have sex with?

Peacunts.

• • •

How does a deaf woman masturbate?

She reads her own lips.

• • •

What's the definition of a slut?

A girl who has to get tight before she gets loose.

• • •

What do you call a dozen vibrators?

Toys for Twats.

• • •

Herman's wife tells him to be home by six sharp or else. She's tired of his staying out late every night, bowling with his friends.

Herman's secretary, Alice, is a real knockout. At ten to six she says to Herman, "Could you drive me home?"

Her apartment, Herman remembers, is at least ten minutes out of his way. But, being a good boss, he agrees, though he knows his wife will be mad. As they're driving to his secretary's place, they pass the supermarket.

Alice wants to stop and pick up just a couple of items, won't take a minute. Reluctantly, Herman agrees. Twenty minutes later, they pull up in front of Alice's apartment building. Herman is already half an hour late. Alice invites him upstairs—for just one drink, she claims. Herman can't think of any way out of it, so he agrees—just one drink.

Alice makes them a drink. Then another. Then another. Before long, Herman and his secretary are in bed, fucking their brains out. Hours later, he wakes up and looks at the clock. It's four in the morning.

"Oh,my God," Herman cries. "My wife is going to kill me. I was supposed to be home by six!"

Then Herman gets a great idea. He pours baby powder over his hands, lots of it.

He dresses and rushes on home. He is immediately confronted by his wife, who is very angry.

"And just where the hell have you been?" she asks.

Herman replies, "I gave my secretary a ride home,

she invited me up for a drink, and we ended up in bed together."

Herman's wife notices the baby powder on her husband's hands and says, "Don't lie to me, Herman. You were out bowling all night!"

"Yes, honey," Herman says. "I was."

• • •

Why do elephants have four feet?

Because two feet won't satisfy a lady elephant.

• • •

What's the definition of a rubber?

Around the cock protection.

• • •

What did the whore get when she slept with the judge?

An honorable discharge.

GROSS GAY AND LESBIAN JOKES

What do you get when you cross fifty lesbians and fifty politicians?

A hundred people who don't do dick.

• • •

Bruce came home from work. His lover, Stanley, said to him, "Oh, Brucie, it feels like I've got something stuck in my asshole. Could you take a look?"

Bruce told Stanley to bend over and took a peek up his lover's blowhole. "I don't see anything up there, Stanley."

Stanley replied, "But there is, I can feel it. Stick a finger in there and maybe you'll feel something."

Bruce complied. "I still don't feel anything, Stanley."

Stanley said, "I know something's up there, I can feel it. Stick another finger up there."

Bruce did, sticking two fingers up Stanley's poop chute. Bruce said, "I still don't feel anything."

Stanley said, "Try putting your hand up there."

Bruce shoved his hand way up Stanley's asshole. When he pulled it out, there was a thousand-dollar Rolex watch on his wrist.

Amazed, Bruce said, "What the hell—"

Stanley said, "Happy birthday to you, happy birthday to you . . ."

What kind of bread do faggots like best?

Humpernickel.

• • •

Little Johnny came home from school, crying his eyes out. His mother said, "Johnny, why are you crying?"

Johnny replied, "Because Stevie called me a sissy!"

"What did you do?" his mother asked.

"I hit him with my purse!"

• • •

What do you call a gay fruit?

A fig-git.

• • •

A rabbi and a priest accidentally walk into a gay bar. They are barely seated when a young man walks over to the priest and asks him for the next dance.

Horrified, the priest turns to the rabbi and says, "Please help me out of this, Sidney."

The rabbi whispers something into the faggot's ear, and he walks away. The priest, visibly relieved, asks the rabbi, "What did you say to him, Sid?"

The rabbi replies, "I told him we were on our honeymoon."

• • •

A fag walks into a sex shop and starts looking over the rubber dildoes. He sees one he really likes: a twelve-inch black one. Pointing to the huge rubber dick, he says to the clerk, "I'll take that one."

The clerk says, "Should I wrap it up?"

The fag replies, "No thanks. I'll eat it here."

• • •

What do you call a gay masochist?

A sucker for punishment.

• • •

A gay man goes to see his doctor, who tells him, "The news is bad, very bad. I'm afraid you've tested positive. You've got AIDS."

"That's terrible," the gay guy says. "What should I do?"

"Go to Mexico," the doctor advises.

"Mexico?" the gay guy asks.

"That's right," the doctor says. "Drink the water, eat lots of Mexican food, especially the raw fruit and vegetables."

"Will that cure my AIDS?"

"No, but it will definitely teach you what your asshole is for."

• • •

So Joel and Evan are walking along the beach when they spot a bottle half-buried in the sand. Upon rubbing it a genie pops out.

The genie looks them over and says, "Are you two guys gay?"

Joel and Evan admit that they are, so the genie says, "To speak the plain truth, I don't like gay people. But you've freed me from this bottle after thousands of years, so I'm supposed to grant you three wishes. Instead, I'll grant you one wish. Think carefully, and when you're ready, just make the wish."

The genie disappears. Joel and Evan return to their hotel room.

A few minutes later, the door bursts open and a dozen white-sheeted men storm into the place.

"We're the KKK," one of them says, "and we're gonna string you-all up!"

Sure enough, the klansmen start putting ropes around the faggots' necks.

"Joel," Evan says to his lover, "this might be a good time to make that wish."

Evan replies, "I already did."

"What do you mean, you already did?" Joel asks as he feels the rope tighten around his neck.

"I wished that we could both be hung like niggers," Evan says.

• • •

What is the AIDS hotline number?

1-800-TOO-LATE.

• • •

What do lawyers and male prostitutes have in common?

They both make their living fucking people up the ass.

• • •

What do lesbians give their lovers on Christmas?

Gift-wrapped batteries.

• • •

What's the most popular comic book in Greenwich Village?

Teenage Mutant Ninja Gerbils.

• • •

What's the difference between AIDS and golf?

In golf one bad hole won't kill you.

• • •

What's the difference between a fag and a refrigerator?

A refrigerator doesn't fart when you pull the meat out.

• • •

How do you know when you're in a dyke bar?

Even the pool table doesn't have any balls.

• • •

How many fags does it take to mug an old lady?

Five—four to hold her down and one to do her hair.

• • •

What is "71"?

"69" with two fingers up your ass.

• • •

How did the young guy know he was bisexual?

He was only half in Earnest.

• • •

What happened to the gay Eskimos?

They got Kool-AIDS.

• • •

How do faggots play Russian roulette?

They pass around six boys, and one of them has AIDS.

• • •

Two Polish fags meet in a gay bar and go home together. They spend the night butt-fucking and sucking each other off.

The next morning, one of the Polish fags gets dressed to leave. He extends his hand to the other Polish fag for a handshake.

"Are you crazy?" the second Polish fag exclaims. "I heard you can get AIDS that way!"

• • •

The residents of the small Southern town urge the sheriff to arrest the local homosexual. Seems he's been propositioning all the teenage boys in town.

The sheriff dutifully arrests the fag and says to him, "Okay, homo. You got fifteen minutes to blow this town!"

The homosexual says, "I'll need at least two hours."

• • •

What do you call a woman with PMS and ESP?

A bitch who thinks she knows everything.

• • •

The gynecologist says to the woman, "Well, Miss Flick. I've studied all the results of the tests we've done, and it's my conclusion that you don't have PMS."

"Then what's wrong with me?" the woman asks.

The gynecologist says, "Basically, you're just a bitch."

• • •

What do you call all the useless meat around a pussy?

A woman.

• • •

What do fags eat at Chinese restaurants?

Sum Hung Guy.

• • •

What do AIDS and Vitamin C have in common?

You get them both from fruit juice.

• • •

What's the favorite sport in gay bars?

Cockfighting.

• • •

Why did Clinton get the gay vote?

Because fags don't like Bush.

• • •

What did the romantic fag say to the stranger at the gay bar?

"May I push in your stool?"

• • •

What do you call an AIDS hospital in Atlanta?

Sick Fags Over Georgia.

• • •

What's a faggot's favorite sitcom?

Leave It, It's Beaver.

• • •

What do lesbians and vegetarians have in common?

They don't eat meat.

• • •

A doctor says to his male patient, "I've got good news, and I've got bad news.The bad news is you show signs of being a homosexual."

"With bad news like that, what could be good news?" the patient asks.

"The good news is," the doctor replies, "I think you're cute."

• • •

Gay guy tries to enlist in the Marines. The recruiter, a tough old sergeant, looks suspiciously at the gay guy.

"You don't look so tough," the recruiter says. "Do you think you could ever kill a man?"

"Yes, but it would take a couple of weeks," the fag replies.

• • •

How are a lesbian and a food critic alike?

Both love to eat out.

• • •

How did k.d. lang win a Grammy award?

She licked the competition.

• • •

What did one lesbian frog say to the other lesbian frog?

They're right. You *do* taste like chicken.

• • •

Why did the fag boy leave home?

He didn't like the way he was being reared.

• • •

Why did the fag boy return home?

He couldn't leave his brother's behind.

• • •

What do you call an anal artist?

Pick-ass-o.

• • •

What's the definition of a homosexual?

A guy who's a bum fuck.

• • •

What does AIDS stand for?

Adios Infected Dick Sucker.

• • •

Why was the homosexual kicked out of heaven?

He blew all the prophets.

• • •

Why did the fag shove sunflower seeds up his ass?

Because gerbils have to eat, too.

• • •

What's the definition of frustration?

A blind lesbian in a fish market.

• • •

What do you call a lesbian dinosaur?

Lick-a-lot-a-puss.

• • •

Did you hear about the queer who got fired from the sperm bank?

He was drinking on the job.

• • •

Why is San Francisco like granola?

Once you get past the fruits and nuts, all you have left is the flakes.

• • •

What do you call a lesbian from Alaska?

A Klondyke.

• • •

How come there were no athletes from Australia at the Gay Olympics?

They couldn't get out of Sidney.

• • •

Why did the Catholic fag enjoy going to Mass?

Afterward, he felt like a new man.

• • •

What's a fag's worst nightmare?

A blow job from Jeffrey Dahmer.

• • •

What do you call a fag working at Fannie Farmer?

A fudge packer.

• • •

What do fags and hamburgers have in common?

Hot meat between two buns.

• • •

What's the definition of a gay murder?

Homo-cide.

• • •

How does a faggot fake an orgasm?

He throws hot yogurt on your back.

• • •

A gay guy says to his friend, who's straight, "Let's play hide-and-seek. If you find me, I get to give you a blow job."

"What if I can't find you?" his straight friend asks.

The fag says, "I'll be behind the couch."

• • •

Hear about the two gay judges?

They decided to try each other.

• • •

A fag goes to a proctologist. The doctor is young and handsome. The fag is clearly in love.

"Bend over," the proctologist says to his faggy patient. The fag does so.

The doctor shines his little light up the faggot's asshole. He's amazed at what he sees.

The doctor says, "I don't know how to tell you this, but you've got a dozen roses up your asshole."

The fag says, "Read the card first!"

• • •

What do you call one hundred fags and a Jew?

A musical.

• • •

How do you punish a faggot?

Put SUPER GLUE in his K-Y Jelly.

• • •

What is AIDS?

A disease that makes vegetables out of fruits.

• • •

What do you call a fag with a hard-on?

A can opener.

• • •

Why do faggots want to join the Navy?

Because the Navy makes men.

• • •

How do you know when your doctor is gay?

He grabs your shoulders when he sticks the thermometer up your ass.

• • •

How did everyone know the bodybuilder was gay?

He got caught pumping Myron.

• • •

Why did the gay poker game turn into an orgy?

The queens were wild.

• • •

The state trooper was patrolling a country road when he spotted a man tied to a tree—stark naked.

"What happened here?" the trooper asked the naked man.

"Well," the man said, "I picked up a hitchhiker, and as soon as he got into the car, he pulled a gun, took my money, made me take off all my clothes, then did this to me!"

The trooper unzipped his fly and said, "Boy, this just ain't your day."

• • •

The fag had a bad case of hemorrhoids, so his doctor gave him suppositories. When it came time to use them, though, the fag was nervous about putting them in properly. So he bent over, looking through his legs at the mirror to get a better view of his ass-hole.

Suddenly, his dick started getting hard and blocked his view of the mirror.

"Oh, stop it," the fag said to his penis. "It's only me."

• • •

How do straight men suddenly turn gay?

They get sucked into it.

• • •

How many queers does it take to screw in a lightbulb?

None. Queers don't screw. They butt-fuck.

• • •

Bruce and Stanley were returning home from their favorite gay bar late one night. Bruce said, "Are you hungry, Stanley?"

"Now that you mention it," Stanley replied, "I am."

Just at that point, a flasher bounded out from the alley and exposed himself.

"Perfect," Bruce said. "Take-out food!"

• • •

Why are there so many homosexuals in the world?

Because there's a sucker born every minute.

• • •

Why was the gay Mexican fisherman so depressed?

He couldn't stop thinking about the Juan who got away.

• • •

A swishy fag walks into the toughest, meanest truck stop on the highway. Sitting on his shoulder is a canary.

The place is full of burly, muscular truckers. The fag announces, "Whoever can guess the weight of the canary on my shoulder gets to take me into the back room and fuck me up the ass!"

One trucker calls out, "Five hundred pounds."

The fag says, "Folks, we have a winner!"

• • •

Two faggots are driving home one night in a blinding rainstorm and don't see the truck ahead of them stop short. The fag behind the wheel crashes into the truck. The trucker climbs out of the rig, hopping mad, and begins screaming at the gay driver.

"You stupid son-of-a-bitch, you drive like shit! You can kiss my rosy red ass!"

The gay driver says to his companion, "Thank God. He wants to settle out of court."

• • •

How do you make a fruit cordial?

Pat him on the ass.

• • •

Why was the fag disappointed when he finally arrived in London?

He found out Big Ben was actually a clock.

• • •

What did one gay sperm say to the other gay sperm?

"How am I supposed to find the egg in all this shit?"

• • •

What did the lesbian say as she guided her girl-friend's tongue to her clitoris?

"This bud's for you."

• • •

Bonnie walks into a bar with some time to kill, and orders a beer. When her eyes adjust to the dimness, she realizes with some horror that she's just entered a dyke bar.

Sure enough, a big lezzie spots her and starts coming on to her. She's chagrined to learn that Bonnie is straight.

"Men," the big lezzie snorts. "My dildo can do anything a man can do!"

"Oh yeah?" Bonnie asks. "Let's see it get up and order a round for the house."

• • •

Hear about the gay plastic surgeon?

He hung himself.

• • •

What do you call a bouncer in a gay bar?

A flamethrower.

• • •

Why did the fag join the Navy?

He wanted to be a rear admiral.

• • •

What do you call a fag with a chipped front tooth?

An organ grinder.

• • •

What do you call two fags named Bob?

Oral Roberts.

• • •

How did the two fags in the gay bar settle their argument?

They went out into the alley and exchanged blows.

• • •

Why did the lesbian return home from her European vacation a week early?

She missed her native tongue.

• • •

What's the difference between an elephant and a bull dyke?

A hundred pounds and a flannel shirt.

• • •

The insurance salesman was writing up a policy for the fag. The salesman said, "So you want your policy to be straight life, right?"

"Well," said the fag, "I *would* like to play around on Saturday nights."

• • •

A fag walks into a rough waterfront bar and propositions a sailor. The sailor is straight, so he drags the fag into the alley and beats the living crap out of him.

A policeman walks by and sees the dazed fag lying in the alley. He says to the fag, "Jesus, what happened to you? You're all black and blue. I'd better take you home."

"Oh, don't do that," the fag pleads. "I'll clash with my curtains."

• • •

Hear about the gay mafia Godfather?

The kiss of death includes dinner and dancing.

GROSS ETHNIC JOKES

What's the difference between a Polish woman and a mosquito?

A mosquito stops sucking when you bash its head in.

• • •

What's the difference between Martin Luther King Day and St. Patrick's Day?

On St. Patrick's Day, people *want* to be Irish.

• • •

How did they break up the Million Man March?

They dropped job applications from a helicopter.

• • •

Who was the one man missing from the Million Man March?

The auctioneer.

• • •

What's black, three miles long, and smelly?

The line at the welfare office.

• • •

What did the Polack say when he found a milk carton in the grass?

"Look—a cow's nest!"

• • •

What do you call a Polack with half a brain?

Gifted.

• • •

Why wasn't the Polack worried when his car was stolen?

He got the license plate number.

• • •

Why did the Polish woman take swimming lessons?

She wanted to be a hooker in Venice.

• • •

What's one job they don't have in Poland?

Mind reader.

• • •

Why couldn't the Polack get a job as the town idiot?

He was overqualified.

• • •

Hear about the black guy who suffered from insomnia?

He kept waking up every few days.

• • •

What's the most popular booth at the Polish carnival?

Guess Your Age—$1.00

• • •

Hear about the Polish sky diver?

He was killed when his snorkel and flippers failed to open.

• • •

Hear about the new Polish parachute?

It opens on impact.

• • •

How do you make a WASP laugh on Monday?

Tell him a joke on Friday.

• • •

The Polish airliner was in trouble. "Mayday, Mayday," the pilot radioed to the tower.

"You're cleared to land," the radar tower came back. "Can you give us your height and position?"

"Well," the Polish pilot replies, "I'm five foot nine and I'm sitting in the front of the plane."

• • •

Hear about the Greek and the Polack who jumped off the Empire State Building?

The Greek guy was killed. The Polack got lost.

• • •

What do most of the patients in Irish hospitals have in common?

They were all IRA explosives experts.

• • •

A man walks out of a house in Belfast. Another man walks up to him and sticks a gun to his head, saying, "Are you a Catholic or a Protestant?"

The first guy is afraid of getting shot if he says the wrong thing. He says, "As a matter of fact, I'm neither. I'm Jewish."

The gunman says, "Hell, I must be the luckiest Arab in Belfast tonight!"

• • •

A Catholic goes to confession. He says to the priest, "Bless me, Father, for I have sinned. I had sex with a married woman."

"That is a very bad sin," the priest says. "You must tell me who she was."

"I can't do that, Father," the man replies. "It wouldn't be right."

"Was it Mary Stevens?"

"No."

"Was it Patty Phillips?"

The man shakes his head. "Please, Father, don't make me tell."

"If you won't tell me, then you will have to do penance. Ten Hail Marys and fifty Our Fathers."

The priest sends him away. Outside, the man spots his friend, who asks him, "Did you tell him?"

"Yes."

"What did you get?"

"Ten Hail Marys, fifty Our Fathers, and a couple of great leads."

• • •

What's the best way to grow dope?

Plant a Polack.

• • •

Why did doctors stop circumcising black babies?

They were throwing away the best part.

• • •

What is PREPARATION H?

Toothpaste for Polacks.

• • •

Why aren't Jewish American Princesses ever attacked by sharks?

Professional courtesy.

• • •

Why are elephants and Jewish mothers alike?

Neither one ever forgets.

• • •

How would you call Mike Tyson if he had no arms or legs?

"Hey, nigger . . ."

• • •

What do black men and sperm have in common?

Only one in two million works.

• • •

How do they advertise BMWs in Harlem?

"You stole the radio—now steal the car!"

• • •

How do you get a dozen Mexicans out of a VW?

Throw in a bar of soap.

• • •

Hear about the redneck who died and left his wife a trust fund?

She couldn't touch the money till she was fourteen.

• • •

How do they make Polish sausage?

From retarded pigs.

• • •

How many Polacks does it take to have a shower?

Six—one to lie in the bathtub and five to piss on him.

• • •

What's the difference between taxes and a Jewish American Princess?

Taxes suck.

• • •

Why did the Polish woman have an abortion?

She couldn't be sure the baby was hers.

• • •

What's the difference between Ted Kennedy and the Polish Army?

Ted Kennedy has at least one confirmed kill.

• • •

What do you call six Italian women in a hot tub?

Gorillas in the mist.

• • •

What do you call an Arab with a goat under one arm and a sheep under the other?

Bisexual.

• • •

How does a Greek firing squad line up?

One behind the other.

• • •

What was the name of the guy who was half Polish and half Chinese?

Sum Dum Fuk.

• • •

What was the name of the Chinese shoe salesman?

Wing Tip Shoo.

• • •

What do you call a fat Oriental?

A chunk.

• • •

Where do Puerto Ricans go for family outings?

Spick-nics.

• • •

What's the definition of a Texan?

A Mexican on his way to Oklahoma.

• • •

A white woman is out in a singles bar with her friends. "Ya know, tonight, just this once, I want to fuck a nigger," she says. Sure enough, a good-looking one comes in, she picks him up, takes him to her place. She strips naked and is lying on the bed and says, "C'mon, big boy. Do what you do best." The black guy grabs her color TV set and runs out the door.

• • •

Why do Puerto Ricans watch baseball?

They love to run and steal.

• • •

What do you call a white baby with wings?

An angel.

• • •

What do you call a black baby with wings?

A bat.

• • •

A Chinese census taker is going from house to house, taking census. He comes to the first house and asks its occupant, "You Lun Yang?" The owner nods his head, the Chink census taker checks his name off. At the second house, he asks the homeowner, "You Shing Lee?" The owner nods his head, the Chink census taker checks his name off, too. At the third house, he asks the homeowner, "You Foo King?" The owner says, "No, watching TV."

• • •

Why were there fifteen thousand Mexicans at the Alamo?

They only had two pickup trucks.

• • •

Why do Mexicans wear mustaches?

They want to look like their mothers.

• • •

Why do Mexicans eat refried beans?

They fucked them up the first time.

• • •

What's the slowest thing in the world?

A Mexican funeral with one set of jumper cables.

• • •

Why don't Italians have pimples?

They slide off.

• • •

What's the difference between an Italian girl and a pizza?

There's less cheese on a pizza.

• • •

What do you get when you cross a nigger with a Puerto Rican with a wop?

I don't know. It's so dirty you don't want to get near it.

• • •

New York City is being plagued by thousands and thousands of rats. The mayor offers a million dollars to anyone who can get rid of all the rats. One day, a man shows up at City Hall in a moving van. Inside is a huge green rat, the size of a car. The man says, "I can get rid of all the rats in New York City." The mayor says, "If you can, I'll give you a million dollars."

The man releases the big green rat. It goes into the city, one borough at a time, and eats all the little rats in three days, ridding New York City of all the rats.

The mayor is thrilled. He hands the green rat's owner a check for a million dollars.

The mayor says to the guy, "Listen, you know where I can get a big, green nigger?"

• • •

What do you call a white guy surrounded by five black men?

Coach.

• • •

What do you call a white guy surrounded by ten black men?

The quarterback.

• • •

What do you call a white guy surrounded by five thousand black men?

Warden.

• • •

What do you call a white guy with one black man?

Parole officer.

• • •

What's the difference between blacks and snow tires?

Snow tires don't scream when you throw chains on them.

• • •

What do you get when you cross an Indian with a Jew?

Chief So-Sioux-Me.

• • •

What do you say to a well-dressed black man?

"Will the defendant please rise."

• • •

What's long and hard on a black man?

Third grade.

• • •

What is the most confusing day in Harlem?

Father's Day.

• • •

How many niggers does it take to shingle a roof?

Depends how thin you slice them.

• • •

What do you get when you cross a nigger with a Puerto Rican?

Someone who's too lazy to steal.

• • •

Why do Jews love skinny women?

So when they marry them, they can buy smaller rings.

• • •

Why don't black babies play in sandboxes?

Because the cats keep covering them up.

• • •

What do you call a black skindiver?

Jacques Custodian.

• • •

How do you kill an Italian?

Smash the toilet seat over his head while he's getting a drink of water.

• • •

Why did God invent orgasms?

So Italians would know when to stop fucking.

• • •

Did you hear about the queer Irishman?

He preferred women over whiskey.

• • •

What is black and shines in the dark?

Oakland.

• • •

What do you get when you cross a nigger and a chink?

A car thief who can't drive.

• • •

What do you get when you cross a Jew and a Gypsy?

A chain of empty stores.

• • •

Why do niggers smell so bad?

So blind people can hate them, too.

• • •

How do you brainwash an Italian?

Give him an enema.

• • •

Why wasn't Christ born in Italy?

Because they couldn't find three wise men and a virgin.

• • •

How do you get an Italian out of a bathtub?

Turn on the water.

• • •

Hear about the fat Italian who was into S&M?

Spaghetti & meatballs.

• • •

Why does Mexico have such a lousy Olympic team?

If they can swim, jump, or run they're already here.

• • •

What did Abraham Lincoln say after the wild party?

"I freed the what?"

• • •

What goes clop clop bang bang clop clop?

An Amish drive-by shooting.

• • •

Where do black people hang out in the South?

From a branch on a tree.

• • •

Did you hear about the two gay Irishmen?

Patrick Fitzjohn and John Fitzpatrick.

• • •

What do you call four niggers in a Cadillac?

Grand theft auto.

• • •

What's the difference between a golf pro and a Jew?

A golf pro gives tips.

• • •

Why would niggers make good astronauts?

They always say, "Yes NASA, no NASA. . . ."

• • •

How are Jews and crime alike?

Both don't pay.

• • •

Did you hear about the Negro who locked his keys in the car?

Took him all day to get his family out.

• • •

How do you know Jesse Jackson is black?

When he gets in a car, the oil light goes on.

• • •

What does an Italian helicopter sound like?

Wop-wop-wop-wop.

• • •

What do you call an Oriental voyeur?

A Peking Tom.

• • •

Why are so many black babies illegitimate?

They don't breed well in captivity.

• • •

What do you call white people in Detroit?

Police.

• • •

What's the ASPCA?

A Mexican singles bar.

• • •

Hear about the Negro who suffered from insomnia?

He kept waking up every few days.

• • •

What do you call a credit card for blacks?

African-American Express.

• • •

Two Italians stood on a corner and watched a dog lick his balls. The first Italian said, "Gee, I wish I could do that."

His friend said, "Maybe you'd better ask the dog if it's okay, first."

• • •

How come black kids don't believe in Santa Claus?

They know no white man will come into their neighborhood after dark.

• • •

How come an Italian mother doesn't go to her daughter's wedding?

Somebody has to stay home with the baby.

• • •

Hear about the golfer who killed the Puerto Rican?

He shot a hole in Juan.

• • •

Did you hear about the Jewish Santa Claus?

He comes down the chimney and says, "Ho ho ho. Anybody wanna buy some toys?"

• • •

Why do black people kill each other?

Because they can.

• • •

What's deadlier in Haiti, AIDS or bullets?

Who cares?

• • •

What's a rich man in Haiti?

A Haitian cabdriver in New York.

• • •

What's the difference between a fag and a black man?

A black man doesn't have to tell his mother he's black.

• • •

Can a black man ever become president of the United States?

Yes, if he runs against a Puerto Rican.

• • •

They found proof of black cavemen—they dug up a Cadillac with four payments left on it.

• • •

A black man is in a graveyard and passes a headstone on which is written NOT DEAD, JUST ASLEEP. The black man says to a companion, "He ain't foolin' nobody but hisself."

• • •

Why are there so few Jewish alcoholics?

It dulls the pain.

• • •

What's the biggest Jewish dilemma?

Ham at half price.

• • •

What's the difference between a chess player and a Jewish wife in bed?

Every once in a while, the chess player moves.

• • •

A Jewish youngster asked the boy next door to play with him. The boy answered, "My father says I can't play with you because you're Jewish."

The Jewish boy answered, "Oh, that's all right. We won't play for money."

• • •

Why are there so many single Jewish girls?

They haven't met their Dr. Right.

• • •

A white guy robs a bank, gets caught, and gets a long jail term. When he gets to the prison, he's put in a cell with a huge black guy.

The black dude sizes up his new white cellmate and says, "Hey, white boy. You got a choice. What you wanna be, the husband or the wife?"

The white guy, who's a little unsure, says, "Well, I guess I'll be the husband."

The black guy says, "Fine. Now get over here and suck your wife's dick."

• • •

Why would rednecks rather not have sex with their sisters?

They don't want to get involved with their relatives.

• • •

How are black families and white families different?

In black families the father runs away from home.

• • •

What's the best thing about the Japanese Mafia?

When they take you for a ride, you get great mileage.

• • •

Why did the black man cut himself shaving?

He got excited when he heard he'd been promoted to the fourth grade.

• • •

What was the first Israeli settlement?

Six cents on the dollar.

• • •

What kind of workers do they have in Ethiopia?

Blue cholera and white cholera.

• • •

What's the one thing they don't need in Ethiopia?

After-dinner mints.

• • •

What does a Puerto Rican kid get for his fifteenth birthday?

Bail.

• • •

What's a seven-course dinner in Korea?

Six puppies and a pound of rice.

• • •

How do you get one hundred Ethiopians into a Volkswagen?

Throw in a bean.

• • •

What do you call an Ethiopian with a swollen big toe?

A golf club.

• • •

A black man is in church one Sunday morning. He looks up toward heaven and asks, "God, why did you make me so dark?"

God answers, "I made you so dark so that when you're running through the jungle, the sun wouldn't give you sunstroke."

"God," the black man asks, "why did you make my hair so coarse?"

God says, "So when you're running through the jungle, your hair would not get caught in the brambles."

"God?" the black man asks, "why did you make my legs so long?"

"I made your legs long," God answers, "so that when you're chasing an animal through the jungle, you would run very fast."

"Then I guess my next question is, Lord," the black man replies, "what the fuck am I doing in Detroit?"

• • •

What did the McDonald's in Ethiopia serve?

McNothing.

• • •

How do you know when you're in a Mexican restaurant?

The waiter pours the water, then warns you not to drink it.

• • •

A bumper sticker in Tennessee: GUNS DON'T KILL PEOPLE—I DO.

• • •

A sixteen-year-old Italian girl comes home pregnant. Her mother yells at her, "Who did it? Who knocked you up?"

"How do I know?" the girl says. "You wouldn't let me go steady."

• • •

What did the black kid take in high school?

Algebra, history, and overcoats.

• • •

An Italian guy gets a job at a restaurant, cooking chickens on the rotisserie. He loves to sing while he works. He starts singing some Italian opera.

A man comes along and stops, listening to the Italian sing and watching him cook the chicken.

The Italian says, "You stop because you like-a my singing, yes?"

"You sing okay," the man says. "But your monkey's on fire."

• • •

Why did the Jewish mother get kicked off the jury?

She kept insisting *she* was guilty.

• • •

The old Jewish man, Melnick, is on his deathbed. His wife, Sadie, says to him, "Sidney, do you have a last wish?"

Melnick smells the honey cake his wife is baking in the kitchen. He says to his wife, "Maybe just a little piece of that cake you're baking that smells so good."

"I'm sorry, Sidney," his wife says. "That's for after the funeral."

• • •

How come Jesse Jackson decided not to run for president?

His wife got caught posing for *National Geographic.*

• • •

Why did the Italian guy spit in his mother's face?

To put out the fire in her mustache.

• • •

Heard about the guy from Alabama who married his sister?

He was relatively happy.

• • •

Why are black people buried twelve feet under?

Because deep down, they're all good.

• • •

A Japanese man walks into a bar and says to the black bartender, "Give me a gin martini, nigger."

The bartender lectures the Jap about racism in America, saying, "And how would you like it if the shoe were on the other foot. What if you were behind this bar and I came in and said, "Give me a drink, slanteye? What would you say then?"

"I say," replies the Jap, "sorry, we no serve niggers in here."

• • •

What do you get when you cross a word processor and a Jewish American Princess?

A system that won't go down.

• • •

Two black guys meet on a street corner in the middle of Harlem.

The first black guy says, "Hey, did you hear about Tyrone? He died."

"Tyrone died?" asks the second black guy. "Hell, I didn't even know he got arrested!"

• • •

Priest says to a rabbi, "Rabbi, have you ever eaten pork?"

The rabbi answers, "Well, once I gave in to temptation and ate a ham sandwich. Let me ask you something," the rabbi continues. "Have you ever been with a woman?"

The priest says, "Once, two years ago, I broke down and tried the services of a prostitute in my parish."

"And what did you think of it?" the rabbi asks.

"It beats the hell out of a ham sandwich," the priest replies.

GROSS CELEBRITY JOKES

• • • • • • •

What did Nicole say to Ron Goldman?

Bring the glasses over. It won't kill you.

• • •

What do you call a Tupac Shakur cocktail?

Five shots and you're in a wheelchair.

• • •

What did Joey Buttafucco say to O.J.?

"You shoulda had your girlfriend do it."

• • •

Where did O.J. say he was on the night of Nicole's murder?

Waiting to get served at Denny's.

• • •

What do Roseanne Barr and a coke dealer have in common?

Three hundred pounds of crack.

• • •

What's the definition of happiness?

A mosquito on Dolly Parton's left tit.

• • •

What do Jeffrey Dahmer and a taxidermist have in common?

They both mount the dead.

• • •

How did Stevie Wonder pierce his ears?

He answered the stapler.

• • •

How did Roseanne Barr know she was getting fatter?

She hung license plates from her charm bracelet.

• • •

What did Buckwheat, of the Little Rascals, change his name to when he turned Muslim?

Kareem of Wheat.

• • •

What's Woody Allen's favorite movie?

Close Encounters of the Third Grade.

• • •

How did Woody Allen's new girlfriend die?

Crib death.

• • •

What do good Scotch whiskey and Woody Allen's girlfriend have in common?

They're both twelve years old.

• • •

What did Jeffrey Dahmer get when he came home late for dinner?

The cold shoulder.

• • •

Where does Teddy Kennedy wind up after a long night of drinking?

On the senate floor.

• • •

What's the difference between a hooker and Hillary Clinton?

Hillary only gives snow jobs.

• • •

Why does Hillary Clinton always climb on top?

Because Bill can only fuck up.

• • •

A guy's on a desert island with Cindy Crawford. After a year, Cindy gives in and fucks him. They fall in love. Cindy says, "I'll act out whatever fantasy you want." The guy paints a mustache on her and dresses her in a man's suit. They have sex. Cindy asks, "What's the deal with the mustache and suit?" The guy says, "I always wanted to tell another guy I fucked Cindy Crawford."

• • •

George Burns finally decides to go on the Oprah Winfrey Show, but on one condition: He wants to bed down Oprah. Oprah agrees. After the show is over Oprah and George check into a hotel. Both strip naked. Just as Oprah is about to climb on top of George, she notices that he has both of his hands covering his balls.

"George, why are your hands there?" Oprah asks.

"Because the last nigger I fucked took my wallet."

• • •

What do Michael Jackson and K Mart have in common?

They both have boy's pants half-off.

• • •

What's black and white and comes in small cans?

Michael Jackson.

• • •

Why does Stevie Wonder smile all the time?

He doesn't know he's black.

• • •

What do Michael Jackson and a jockey have in common?

Both like to ride four-year-olds.

• • •

How is Roseanne Barr like a bakery?

Roseanne's got a lot of rolls.

• • •

How do you get Michael Jordan to quit playing baseball?

Shoot his mother.

• • •

Why is O.J. Simpson called O.J.?

He beats his wife to a pulp.

• • •

What is Mike Tyson having for breakfast tomorrow?

Ham and eggs and O.J. on the side.

• • •

What does O.J. stand for?

Oh, Jesus, he's got a knife.

• • •

What did Michael Jackson say to O.J. Simpson?

"Don't worry, I'll look after your kids."

• • •

What does O.J. stand for?

Open Jugular.

• • •

Knock, knock. Who's there?
O.J.
O.J. who?
You're on the jury!

• • •

Did you hear O.J.'s getting married again?

He's taking another stab at it.

• • •

What did Ron Goldman say to Nicole at the Pearly Gates?

"Here're your fucking sunglasses."

• • •

What were O.J.'s last words to Nicole?

"Your waiter will be along shortly."

• • •

What's O.J.'s favorite soda?

Diet Slice.

• • •

What was O.J. like in high school?

He cut class all the time.

• • •

What's O.J.'s favorite store?

Sharper Image.

• • •

Michael Jackson needs to get married. So he goes to Lisa Marie Presley and begs, "Oh please, Lisa. Will you marry me?" Lisa agrees, but tells Michael her one condition: "No more nights out with the boys."

• • •

What was Bill Clinton's mistake in the Paula Jones affair?

He didn't get Ted Kennedy to drive her home.

• • •

How many Kennedys does it take to screw in a lightbulb?

Five. One to hold the bulb in the socket, and the other four to get drunk enough for the room to start turning.

• • •

How do you pick up David Koresh's girlfriend?

With a dust buster.

• • •

What did they say after Michael Jackson had plastic surgery?

"He cut off his nose to spite his race."

• • •

What's the difference between Neil Armstrong and Michael Jackson?

One was the first man to do a moonwalk, the other fucks little boys up the ass.

• • •

How come John Wayne Bobbitt could never be a movie star?

Because every time the director yells "Cut!," Bobbitt faints.

• • •

Who was Susan Smith's driving teacher?

Ted Kennedy.

• • •

What is Susan Smith's favorite TV show?

Sea Hunt.

• • •

What killed Jerry Garcia?

Acid indigestion.

• • •

Hear about the new limo service O.J. is starting?

They'll get you to the airport with an hour to kill.

• • •

Why is O.J. moving to Alabama?

The DNA is all the same.

• • •

What's black, sixty years old, and is sitting in O.J's jacuzzi?

Juror Number Seven.

• • •

Why can't Ted Kennedy give blood?

They can't get all the cocktail olives through the tubes.

• • •

Why isn't Washington's Birthday celebrated in Washington, D.C.?

Because a man who can't tell a lie isn't worth remembering.

• • •

This gal is so hot for Tom Cruise and Brad Pitt that she decides to have their likenesses tattooed on her butt, one on each cheek. Her boyfriend is furious but wants to see what they look like.

The girl drops her jeans and sticks out her ass.

Her boyfriend says, "They don't look anything like Tom Cruise or Brad Pitt."

The pair argue, and the girl says she wants a second opinion. When the mailman comes to the door, she proudly displays her newly tattooed cheeks and asks him, "Do you know whose faces these are?"

"No," the mailman says, "but the one in the middle looks just like Willie Nelson."

• • •

How much does Johnny Cochran charge to screw in a lightbulb?

How much you got?

• • •

Why won't Louis Farrakhan run for president?

They don't make bulletproof Cadillacs.

• • •

What do you call a big fat actress?

Moby Roseanne.

• • •

How did Moby Roseanne commit suicide?

She shot herself with a harpoon.

• • •

Why are Michael Jackson's pants so short?

They belong to a ten-year-old.

• • •

What's Michael Jackson's favorite drink?

Seven and Up.

• • •

What is John Wayne Bobbitt's favorite flick?

Return of the Magnificent Seven.

• • •

What did the telephone operator say to John Wayne Bobbitt?

"Sorry, but you've been cut off."

• • •

What did Jeffrey Dahmer say to Lorena Bobbitt?

"I like mustard on mine."

• • •

Why was Lorena Bobbitt arrested?

Shc got caught littering.

• • •

Why is John Wayne Bobbitt like a snowstorm?

They both have six inches on the ground.

• • •

What's O.J.'s best golf move?

A slice.

• • •

What were David Koresh's last words?

"Getting kinda hot in here, ain't it?"

What's a Branch Davidian's favorite dessert?

Toasted marshmallows.

• • •

What's twenty-five years old and gets very little sleep at night?

Paula Barbieri.

• • •

What weighs three hundred pounds and cares about the environment?

Sidney Greenpeace.

• • •

What did the seven dwarfs say when the prince woke Sleeping Beauty?

"Looks like it's back to jerking off."

• • •

What do Roseanne and a football have in common?

Pigskin.

• • •

If Tarzan was an Arab, what would Cheetah be?

Pregnant.

• • •

Why does Stevie Wonder have one black leg and one yellow leg?

His dog is blind, too.

• • •

Why doesn't Roseanne ever wear yellow?

She doesn't want people to think she's a taxi.

• • •

What does Michael Jackson hate about having sex?

Getting the bubble gum off his dick.

• • •

What did God say when he created Minister Louis Farrakhan?

"Holy shit!"

• • •

What do Roseanne and a hollowed-out pumpkin have in common?

They're both heads with nothing inside.

• • •

What did Jerry Garcia say to Elvis when he got to Heaven?

"You're not gonna believe who your daughter just married!"

• • •

What's the difference between Jane Fonda and Bill Clinton?

Jane Fonda went to Vietnam.

• • •

What do Ethiopians and Yoko Ono have in common?

They both live off dead beetles.

• • •

What's the difference between Madonna and a limousine?

Not everyone's been in a limousine.

• • •

What do you call a bathroom for bisexuals?

The Elton John.

• • •

Michael Jackson goes to see his doctor for a checkup. After the examination, the doctor says to him, "Mr. Jackson, have you been having sex with little boys again?"

"Yes," Michael Jackson confesses, "I just can't help myself. But how did you know?"

The doctor replies, "Because you've got a G.I. Joe doll up your ass."

• • •

What do Jeffrey Dahmer and gravediggers have in common?

They both dig dead people's holes.

• • •

What's the difference between Pee Wee Herman and Rodney King?

Pee Wee only beats himself.

• • •

A very rich man suffers a heart attack and is rushed to the hospital. A few days later, his doctor comes to him and says, "I have good news and I have bad news."

"What's the good news?" the rich man wants to know.

"The good news is," the doctor says, "your heart attack isn't as bad as we first thought, and with some rest and a proper diet, you'll recover very nicely."

"That *is* good news," the rich man says. "But what's the bad news?"

"The bad news is," the doctor says, "your wife just fired me and hired another doctor named Kevorkian."

• • •

How does Ted Bundy's family honor his memory?

Every year they put a wreath on a fuse box.

• • •

What did Jodie Foster say to her girlfriend?

"My face or yours?"

• • •

What does Jodie Foster do every day at noon?

She has a box lunch.

• • •

Hear about Evel Knievel's latest stunt?

He's going to run across Somalia with a sandwich tied to his back.

• • •

What do you call Jodie Foster, k.d. lang, and Martina Navratilova?

A ménage à twat.

• • •

What's the difference between Hillary Clinton and a great white shark?

Nail polish.

• • •

What do you get when you cross a cat with Mick Jagger?

A pussy with big lips.

• • •

What's brown and hides in an attic?

The Diarrhea of Anne Frank.

• • •

Why did Maria Shriver marry Arnold Schwarzenegger?

They're trying to breed bulletproof Kennedys.

• • •

Hear about the new special sandwich at McDonald's?

It's called a McJackon—thirty-five-year-old meat between eleven-year-old buns.

• • •

What has two hundred legs and ten teeth?

The front row of a Willie Nelson concert.

• • •

What does Tailhook really stand for?

"Do we have to do it doggy-style again, Admiral?"

• • •

How did Helen Keller's parents punish her?

They stretched Saran Wrap over the toilet.

• • •

How does Helen Keller masturbate?

She gets a manicure.

• • •

Why did Karen Carpenter give her dog away?

It kept trying to bury her.

• • •

Why was Roseanne arrested for drug possession?

Cops found fifty pounds of crack under her dress.

• • •

What do you get when you cross a Jew with Ted Kennedy?

A drunk who buys his booze retail.

• • •

What's so special about the White House elevator?

It's the only thing Hillary Clinton will go down on.

SO GROSS EVEN WE WERE OFFENDED

• • • • • • •

What do the Unabomber and a girl from Alabama have in common?

They were both fingered by a brother.

• • •

What company is the leading manufacturer of vibrators?

Genital Electric.

• • •

What do you call a man who has sex with rabbits?

Elmer Fuck.

• • •

How do you know when your girlfriend is getting too fat?

The guy from Prudential offers her group insurance.

• • •

What's the definition of old age?

When all the girls in your little black book are grandmothers.

Another definition of old age: when you not only can't cut the mustard, you can't even open the jar.

• • •

What did one alligator say to the other alligator after the ValueJet crash in the Everglades?

"Not bad for airline food."

• • •

Why did the Polish burglar break two windows?

One to get in, one to get out.

• • •

How did the Polish dog get a flat nose?

Chasing parked cars.

• • •

What's the easiest way to get into a sex club?

Just come.

• • •

Why did the girl stop dating the cannibal?

He just wanted her for her body.

• • •

What's the definition of Italian ices?

A frozen cesspool.

• • •

How do you know when you have a bad physician?

His office plants are dead.

• • •

How many Arab terrorists does it take to screw in a lightbulb?

None—they just stand around and threaten it.

• • •

What was the first lie ever told?

Adam to Eve: "Eat this apple. It'll make your tits bigger."

• • •

Why are old men like babies?

They like to be Pampered.

• • •

What do you call diapers for old people?

Grampers.

• • •

What's the difference between a slut and a tooth-brush?

You don't let your friends borrow your toothbrush.

• • •

Why are men like microwaves?

They get hot really fast, then go off in thirty seconds.

• • •

Two drunken Polacks come stumbling out of a bar and start pissing in a garden. A cop comes along and starts writing each of them a ticket for public urination.

The cop, writing up the ticket, says to the first Polack, "Where do you live?"

The first Polack is so drunk, he can't remember. He tells the cop, "I don't know."

Exasperated, the cop says to the second Polack, "Where do *you* live?"

The second Polack says proudly, "I live next door to him."

• • •

A tourist couple walk into a bar in a really tough Irish neighborhood in New York's Hell's Kitchen.

The wife says to her husband, "Look, Sidney—there's sawdust on the floor. How quaint!"

"That ain't sawdust, lady," the bartender says, "That's last night's furniture."

• • •

What do you call a black woman with two or more daughters?

The madam.

• • •

Why did the prostitute stop giving blow jobs and become a computer programmer?

There was less down time.

• • •

So the eighty-year-old man is prouder than hell when his twenty-year-old wife gets pregnant.

Nine months to the day, she is rushed to the maternity ward. A few hours later, the nurse comes out and says to the old man, "Congratulations, sir. Your wife just had twins."

The old man says to the nurse, "It just goes to show you—there may be snow on the roof, but there's fire in the furnace!"

"Then you better change your filters," the nurse tells the old man, "because both babies are black."

• • •

What's the best thing about having Alzheimer's Disease?

You can hide your own Easter eggs.

• • •

What are the three words no man wants to hear when he's making love?

"Darling, I'm home."

• • •

A not too bright girl goes to see her gynecologist. She says to him, "Doctor, my boyfriend wants to have anal sex with me. Can I get pregnant this way?"

The doctor says, "Not unless you want to have a lawyer."

• • •

Marvin and Sidney were business partners who were taking turns banging their young secretary. The secretary became pregnant. Nine months later, she gave birth. Marvin went to the hospital first. Sidney arrived ten minutes later.

"Congratulations," Marvin said to his business partner. "She had twins. Unfortunately, mine died."

• • •

What's the definition of a virgin in Alabama?

An ugly second grader.

• • •

What's the difference between a French poodle humping your leg and an elephant humping your leg?

You let the elephant finish.

• • •

A guy is going to Las Vegas for the weekend. His best friend gives him one hundred dollars and says, "Do what you can for me." The following Monday, the friend says, "Welcome home. How'd I do?"

"Great," says the guy. "You got laid."

• • •

What's the best way to fight crime?

Don't vote.

• • •

Undertaker says to the grieving husband, "Should we bury her, embalm her, or cremate her?"

The husband says, "Why take chances? Do all three."

• • •

Did you hear about the deaf gynecologist?

He had to learn how to read lips.

• • •

A man goes to see his doctor with an unusual problem. He tells the doctor, "I was born with five penises."

The doctor says, "That's terrible. How do your pants fit?"

"Like a glove," the man answers.

• • •

What's red and dances?

A baby on a barbecue.

• • •

How do you get rid of child molesters?

Incest-o-cide.

• • •

This guy walks into a bar and says to the bartender, "I'd like a Scotch and soda, and I'd like to buy that douche bag at the end of the bar a drink." The bartender says, "Hey, she's a regular. You can't be talking about her that way." The guy says, "Okay, I'd like to buy that nice young lady at the end of the bar a drink." The bartender says, "That's more like it," and walks up to the girl and asks what she wants to drink.

"Vinegar and water," she says.

• • •

A man is screwing a married woman. They hear a car door slam and realize the husband has come home.

"Quick, jump out the window," the woman says.

Totally naked, the man does just that. Down on the street, the New York City Marathon is in progress. The naked man jumps into the race and starts running along with the rest.

A runner asks the naked man, "Do you always run in the nude?"

"Yes," says the guy.

The runner then asks, "And do you always run naked wearing a condom?"

"Yes," the naked guy says. "It looked like rain today."

• • •

What do you call ten thousand lawyers in the Grand Canyon?

A good start.

• • •

What did Bill Clinton say to Hillary after sex?

"I'll be home in a half hour."

• • •

What does an eighty-year-old woman taste like?

Depends.

• • •

What do you call blondes in a freezer?

Frosted Flakes.

• • •

What do you call two guys with no arms and no legs who are hanging over a window?

Curt and Rod.

• • •

What's the difference between a lawyer and a spermatozoa?

A spermatozoa has a one in six million chance of becoming a human being.

• • •

A guy walks into his doctor's office. He says, "D-D-D-D-octor. I-I-I-I-I have this bad stutter that won't go away."

The doctor replies, "All right. Let's give you a physical examination and we'll see what the problem is."

During the exam, the doctor discovers that the stutterer has the longest penis he's ever seen. The doctor then explains to the man a rare and delicate operation that might stop his stuttering: the shortening of the man's penis. The man agrees to it. The doctor anesthetizes and then successfully operates on the man. The man wakes up and discovers that his stutter is gone. "Doc! How can I ever thank you?" The doctor replies; "D-d-d-d-d-d-d-d-d-d-d-on't mention it."

• • •

Hear of the movie about Jeffrey Dahmer?

Honey, I Ate the Kids.

• • •

What do you get when you cross a chicken with a hooker?

A chicken that lays you.

• • •

What do a taxidermist and a pervert have in common?

They both mount sheep.

• • •

What kind of floor cleanser do prostitutes use?

Mop 'n' Blow.

• • •

Why do women have two sets of lips?

So they can piss and moan at the same time.

• • •

The old lady in Miami Beach happened upon a handsome older man soaking up the sun on the beach. She said to him, "So, tell me about yourself."

The man answered, "Well, I just got out of prison, where I served thirty years. I took a knife and stabbed my wife a hundred times, then cut her body into a bunch of little pieces and set them on fire."

The old lady asks, "So, you're single?"

• • •

Why are men better off than women?

They marry later and die earlier.

• • •

What happened when the Mafia don made love to the fat woman?

He got bumped off.

• • •

Two elderly men are sitting and one says, "TGIF."
The other says, "What does that mean?"
"Thank God, It's Friday."
The other says, "SHIT."
"What does that mean?"
"So Happens It's Thursday."

• • •

What's the definition of a loser?

A guy who puts a seashell to his ear and gets a busy signal.

• • •

Another definition of a loser?

A guy who gets AIDS from a wet dream.

• • •

What's the ultimate definition of a loser?

A guy who gets shipwrecked on a desert island . . . with his wife.

• • •

A guy goes hunting for bear. After a few hours in the forest, he finally sees a giant grizzly. He gets the bear in his rifle's sight and is about to pull the trigger when he feels a tap on his shoulder. It's the bear.

"Well, buddy," the bear says. "I can rip your head off or you can suck my dick. What's it gonna be?"

"I'll suck your dick, Mr. Bear."

The next day, the hunter is in the forest when he sees the same bear in his rifle's sights. He's about to pull the trigger when he feels a tap on his shoulder.

"Well buddy," the bear says. "I can rip your head off or I'll fuck you in the ass. What's it gonna be?"

"Oh, fuck me in the ass, Mr. Bear."

The next day, the hunter is in the forest again, waiting to catch up with that bear. He sees the bear again in his rifle's sights and is about to pull the trigger when he feels a tap on his shoulder.

"Buddy, you ain't here for huntin'."

• • •

Then there was the proctologist who used two fingers whenever his patients wanted a second opinion.

• • •

What's meaner than a pit bull with AIDS?

The guy that gave it to him.

• • •

Mike and Sam head down to Florida for spring break. Neither of them are what could be described as good-looking, but somehow, every time they go down to the beach, Sam always leaves with a beautiful woman, while Mike returns to the motel room alone.

"How do you manage to score all the time?" Mike wants to know.

"It's easy," Sam tells his friend. "Each day when I leave for the beach, I put on the tightest bathing suit I can find and stuff a cucumber in it."

The next day, Mike hurries down to the store and buys the tightest bathing suit he could find and a cucumber. After two days, though, he is still bombing out, while Sam is scoring each time. Frustrated, Mike asks Sam why he isn't scoring.

"The trunks are fine," Sam tells his friend, "but tomorrow, try putting the cucumber in *front*."

• • •

A Jew, an Indian, and a black all die and approach the Pearly Gates at the same time.

The Jew says, "St. Peter, I've suffered discrimination my entire life. Will I find any in heaven?"

"No," St. Peter says. "All you have to do is answer one question, and you will find peace and tranquillity for all eternity. Spell God."

"G-O-D," answers the Jew, and is admitted into heaven.

The Indian approaches St. Peter and says, "All my life I have lived on the reservation, and have known discrimination. Will there be prejudice in heaven?"

"No," St. Peter responds. "If you answer this one question correctly, peace and tranquillity will be yours for all eternity. Spell God."

"G-O-D," the Indian says, and is admitted into heaven.

The black man says to St. Peter, "All my life I have lived in the ghetto and have suffered discrimination. Will I find any in heaven?"

"No," St. Peter says. "Answer this one question correctly, and peace and tranquillity will be yours for all eternity. Spell cross-pollination."

• • •

What's the definition of pussy-whipped?

Being impotent and afraid to tell your pregnant wife.

• • •

A six-year-old boy walks into a saloon and says to the barmaid, "Give me a Scotch on the rocks."

The barmaid says, "A Scotch on the rocks? You're just a kid. Do you want to get me in trouble?"

"Maybe later," the kid replies. "In the meantime, I'd like that drink."

• • •

What's the difference between like and love?

Spit or swallow.

• • •

Hear about the Jewish American Princess's baby?

She was breast-fed by the caterer.

• • •

How do you tease your houseplants?

Water them with ice cubes.

• • •

What do you call sushi in Alabama?

Bait.

• • •

What's the best thing about dating a homeless woman?

It's easy to persuade her to spend the night with you.

• • •

What's the difference between a catfish and a lawyer?

One is a bottom-feeding, shit-sucking scavenger, the other is a fish.

• • •

"I just found out that my wife is a lesbian," Al told the bartender.

"That's too bad," the bartender said. "Are you going to divorce her?"

"Nope," Al replied. "I'm crazy about her girlfriend!"

• • •

Ed's wife is so depressed he takes her to see a psychiatrist. Ed waits outside while the shrink checks her over. Later, he calls Ed into his office.

"In my opinion," the shrink tells Ed, "your wife is depressed because she's not getting enough sex."

"What can I do?" Ed asks.

"I recommend that your wife have sex at least ten times a month," the shrink advises.

"Fair enough," says Ed. "Put me down for two."

• • •

Then there was the guy whose wife was ailing, so he took her to see the doctor. The doctor was shocked by her appearance. He said, "I don't like the looks of your wife."

"Neither do I," said her husband, "but she's great with the kids."

• • •

What's the definition of sex drive?

A condition that begins in puberty and ends at marriage.

• • •

"So let me get this straight," the prosecutor says to the defendant. "You came home from work early and found your wife in bed with a strange man?"

"That's correct," responds the defendant.

"Upon which," says the prosecutor, "you took out a gun and shot your wife, killing her."

"That's correct," the defendant replies.

"Then my question is," says the prosecutor, "why did you shoot your wife and not her lover?"

The defendant shrugs. "It seemed easier than shooting a different man every day."

• • •

Why does the Ku Klux Klan like to go surfing with black folks?

They get to hang ten.

• • •

What do you call a Mexican whore who doesn't charge?

A free-holey.

• • •

What's pink and black and hairy and sits on a wall?

Humpty Cunt.

• • •

What's the difference between having a job for ten years and being married for ten years?

After ten years, a job still sucks.

• • •

What's the hardest part of doing a sex change from a man to a woman?

Inserting the anchovies.

• • •

What's white and can be found in a woman's panties?

Clitty litter.

• • •

"Yesterday I came home from work early and found my wife in bed with my best friend," Nick said to the bartender.

"What did you do?" the bartender asked.

"I hit him on the nose with a newspaper and locked him in the basement."

"What good did that do?" asked the barkeep.

"Not much," Nick replied, "but he knew I meant business when I didn't give him his Kibbles and Bits!"

• • •

What's the difference between a woman of forty and a man of forty?

The forty-year-old woman thinks about having kids, and the forty-year-old man thinks about dating them.

• • •

How do you know when your girlfriend is too skinny?

Her shadow weighs more than she does.

• • •

For months, Mona nagged her husband Ollie to take her to the country club so she could learn to play golf. He finally agreed, and off she went with a set of clubs. That afternoon, Mona walked into the bar, grimacing with pain.

"So, did you enjoy your game of golf?" Ollie wanted to know.

"It was horrible," Mona told her husband. "I got stung by a bee."

"Where?"

"Between the first and second holes," she said.

"Sounds to me," Ollie replied, "like your stance was too wide."

• • •

How do you know when your girlfriend is too fat?

She tries to walk down into the Grand Canyon and gets stuck.

• • •

Why is a fat woman like a moped?

They're both fun to ride until your friends see you.

• • •

What happened to the woman who went out fishing with ten men?

She came home with a red snapper.

• • •

What's a JAP's favorite book?

The Naked and the Dead.

• • •

Little Ronnie is jerking off in the bathroom when his mother walks in on him. She says, "What you're doing is wrong, Ronnie. Nice boys save it for when they're married."

A week later, Ronnie's mother asks him, "So, how are you doing with that problem we talked about last week?"

"Great, Mom," Ronnie says. "I've already saved a gallon!"

• • •

Why won't a woman win the Indianapolis 500?

She always stops to ask directions.

• • •

George is a bigshot lawyer and makes a ton of money. His wife decides she wants a maid, so he hires her one.

The next day, he calls home, and a woman answers.

"Hello," George says. "Are you the new maid?"

"Yes, sir," the maid responds.

"I would like to talk to my wife," George says.

"I'm sorry, sir," the maid says, "but she's in the bedroom having sex with the mailman."

George is furious. He says to the maid, "Having sex with the mailman, huh? Here's what I want you to do. In my study, in the top drawer of my desk, is a gun. It's already loaded. I want you to go into the bedroom and shoot my wife and the mailman."

"I can't do that," the maid says. "I'd go to jail for the rest of my life!"

"No, you won't," George assures her. "I'm the best lawyer in the state. I'll get you off with no problem—and give you ten thousand dollars."

The maid puts down the phone. Still listening, George hears two shots. A moment later, the maid comes back on and says, "Well, I just killed them both like you asked."

"Fine," George says. "Now I want you to take both of the bodies and throw them in the pool."

"Pool?" the maid asks. "There's no pool here."

George says, "Is this 555-6734?"

• • •

All through the movie, Dick hears annoying laughter coming from the row behind him. Finally, he's had enough. He turns in his seat and is shocked to see a German shepherd sitting next to its owner.

The angry man says to the dog's owner, "I can't believe you brought your dog here!"

"Neither can I," says the owner. "He hated the book."

• • •

Steve was making passionate love to a married woman when they both heard a car door slam in the driveway.

"Oh, my God," the cheating wife cried. "My husband! If he catches you here, he'll kill you for sure."

Grabbing his pants, Steve said, "Quick, where's the back door?"

"We don't have one," the wife answered.

"Okay," Steve said. "Then where do you want it?"

• • •

What's black and white and red all over?

A nun with multiple stab wounds.

• • •

How many Polacks does it take to rape a woman?

Three—one to hold her down and the other two to read the instructions.

• • •

"I don't know how to tell you this," the gynecologist said to the coffee shop waitress, "but you've got a tea bag stuck up your vagina!"

The waitress said, "I wonder what I served my last customer. . . . "

• • •

What comes immediately after "69"?

Listerine.

• • •

What's the difference between a pickpocket and a peeping Tom?

One snatches watches, the other watches snatches.

• • •

What has four wheels and flies?

A dead cripple in a wheelchair.

• • •

What's the definition of a cheap date?

Taking an anorexic to dinner.

• • •

What's the definition of gross?

Siamese twins joined at the mouth, and one of them throws up.

• • •

How do you know when you're flying Air Mexico?

After landing, you have to steal your luggage back.

• • •

What did the nymphomaniac say when her dog started licking her face?

"Down boy!"

• • •

What's the definition of plastic surgery?

Cutting up your wife's credit cards.

TRULY SICK JOKES

What's the difference between a dead baby and a bathtub?

You can't fuck a bathtub.

• • •

You know a girl is ugly when . . .

The welcome wagon burns a cross on her lawn.

The neighborhood peeping Tom pulls *down* her shade.

She has her face capped.

She won a malpractice suit—against her parents.

As she leaves the beauty parlor, they ask her to use the back door.

• • •

How does an eighty-year-old man spell sex?

H-E-L-P.

• • •

So the husband says to the divorce judge, "I came home, your honor, and I found my wife in bed with a strange man."

"What did she say?" the judge asks.

"That's what bothers me the most," the husband replies. "She said, 'Well, look who's home. The old blabbermouth. Now the whole neighborhood will know!' "

• • •

"I hear you advertised for a wife," Frank said to Bob.

"Yeah," Bob replied.

"Get a response?" Frank wanted to know.

"Hundreds of them," Bob answered. "They all said, 'Take mine.' "

• • •

The man wakes up in a hospital, groggy.

"Where am I?" he asks an intern.

The intern says, "You had a terrible accident and you're in the hospital. Do you want the good news or the bad news first?"

"I can't feel any worse, so give me the bad news first."

"The bad news is we had to operate. The surgeons amputated both of your feet."

"That's awful. What's the good news?"

"The good news is, the guy in the next bed wants to buy your shoes."

• • •

Then there was the loser who called the suicide hot-line.

They told him he was doing the right thing.

• • •

Hear about the girl who got her good looks from her father?

He was a plastic surgeon.

• • •

What do men and linoleum have in common?

Lay them right the first time and you can walk all over them for years.

• • •

Why does the LAPD leave Dodger games in the middle of the ninth inning?

They want to beat the crowds.

• • •

What do you call a virgin in the South?

A girl who can run faster than her brother.

• • •

Two guys are in the desert, both near death. Both are crawling on their hands and knees looking for food and water. Suddenly, they come upon a dead vulture. "Ah! Dinner!" one says to the other.

"You're gonna eat that?" the other replies. "Look at it . . . it's got maggots crawling all over it, its guts are spilling out. If you eat that, you'll never be able to keep it in."

"I don't care. Food is food." Sure enough, he chows down on the bird. A half-hour passes and the vulture eater admits, "I don't feel so good." He proceeds to vomit up the bird.

"Just what I was waiting for!" his friend exclaims. "A hot dinner!"

• • •

What did the Southern girl say after she lost her virginity?

"Thanks, Daddy."

• • •

Did you hear about the constipated accountant?

He took out his pencil and worked it out.

• • •

How many male sexists does it take to screw in a lightbulb?

None. Let the bitch cook in the dark.

• • •

What do you call a girl with no arms or legs who never comes out of the closet?

Heidi.

• • •

What do you have when you're holding two green balls in your hand?

Kermit's undivided attention.

• • •

What is foreplay in Alabama?

"Hey, sis—you awake?"

• • •

What does the LIRR stand for?

Long Island Rifle Range.

• • •

Old Sam is getting on in years, and unfortunately, his son decides that the oldster must go into a nursing home. Old Sam doesn't want to go, but his son tells him he must.

His first day at the nursing home, Old Sam is given a sponge bath by a beautiful young nurse. Old Sam gets a throbbing hard-on, and the nurse gives him a blow job.

Old Sam calls his son the next day and says, "Son, I love this nursing home and I don't ever want to leave."

The next day, Old Sam is walking down the hallway when he falls down and can't get up. A young male orderly comes along to help him, but instead he pops the old man up the ass.

Old Sam calls his son and says, "I hate this place. Come and take me home."

The son says, "But Dad, yesterday you called and said you loved the place and never wanted to come home."

Old Sam says, "Hell, I only get a hard-on once a year, but I fall down every day!"

• • •

The redneck goes to his father and says, "Pa, I'm gettin' married. She's a virgin." The father says, "Hell, you can't marry her."

"Why not?" the son asks.

"Hell, boy," the father says, "if she ain't good enough for her own kin, she ain't good enough for us."

• • •

What's the definition of a poor redneck?

His house has four flat tires.

• • •

A man goes to a doctor. The doctor tells him, "You've got twelve hours to live." The man goes home to his wife. He says, "I have twelve hours to live. Let's have sex."

The man and his wife do it. They have sex again. Afterward, the husband says to his wife, "Can we do it a third time?"

His wife sighs and says, "All right." The man jumps on his wife again. When they're done, the husband says, "Let's do it a fourth time."

"Listen, darling," his wife says. "I have to get up in the morning. You don't."

• • •

A female midget went into a bar. Just to prove she was friendly, she kissed everybody in the joint.

• • •

What's the difference between a computer and US Air?

A computer crashes less.

• • •

A woman is losing her hair. She goes to a doctor who tells her there's a brand-new male hormone that grows hair. Its one side effect is that there's no way of knowing how much hair it will grow.

The woman risks the side effect and returns to her doctor a few weeks later. He asks, "How's it coming along?"

The woman says, "Fine, except that it makes my balls itch."

• • •

Why did the redneck cross the street?

His cock was in a chicken.

• • •

What do you call midgets cheering at a football game?

A micro-wave.

• • •

What do Saddam Hussein and Little Miss Muffet have in common?

They both want Kurds out of their way.

• • •

How about the ugly girl?

Men only wanted to play dress poker with her.

• • •

A man knocks on the door of an exclusive brothel. Through a small window in the door, the madam says, "What can I do for you, sir?"

"I'd like to get screwed," he answered.

"This is a fancy private club. To join, you must slip a hundred dollars under the door."

The man does so, but the door doesn't open. The madam appears again. The man says, "Hey, I'd like to get screwed."

The madam says, "What, again?"

• • •

An old man goes to his physician. The old man says, "Doc, I don't know what to do."

"What seems to be the problem?" the doctor asks.

"Well," the old man says, "all I do from sunup to sundown is cut a lot of silent farts. What can you suggest?"

The doctor says, holding his nose, "The first thing you need to do is see your ear doctor."

• • •

An Easterner decides to buy a large ranch, sixty acres, in the wilds of Montana.

His first day there, the man answers a knock on the door. Standing outside is a rancher.

"Howdy, neighbor," the rancher says. "I live on the spread next to yours. Was wonderin' if you'd like to come to my party tomorrow night. Gonna be some eats. You like to eat?"

"Sure, I like good eats," the Easterner says.

"Gonna be some dancin', too," the farmer says. "You like to dance?"

"Sure, I like dancing," the Easterner says.

"Gonna be some drinkin', too," the rancher says. "You like to drink?"

"Sure, I like to drink," the Easterner says.

"And then, after that, there's gonna be some good sex. You up for that?"

"Sure, I'm up for that," the Easterner says.

"Then swell," the rancher says. "Come on by to the party tomorrow. Around eight."

"Sounds good," the Easterner says. "What should I wear?"

The rancher says, "Wear anything you want. Ain't gonna be but the two of us."

• • •

Henry and Edna are having their tenth wedding anniversary.

Henry says, "Edna, anything you want for your anniversary is yours. A trip to Paris or to the Bahamas, you got it. A mink coat, another diamond ring, anything you want, it's yours."

"Well," Edna asks, "do you remember the first night you cooked dinner for me, back when we had our first date?"

"Yes," Henry replies. "I made snails in olive oil and garlic."

"Yes," Edna says. "Snails in olive oil and garlic. What I want for our tenth anniversary is for you to cook me the very same dish tonight."

Being a loving husband, Henry runs out and goes straight to a fish market, where he buys a dozen live snails. Then he goes to the grocery store for some olive oil and garlic. While he is there, a gorgeous blonde approaches him and says, "You're the sexiest man I've ever met. I live right upstairs. Let's go back to my apartment, and you can do anything you want to me. Anything."

Henry can hardly believe his good fortune. He goes upstairs with the blonde and they get into bed. He fucks her three times. Then he fucks her between the tits, in the mouth, then fucks her again in the ass before he realizes it's seven in the morning.

Frantic, Henry gathers up his olive oil and garlic and snails and dashes out the door. He runs all the way home, races up the three floors to his apartment, and trips on the last stair. The bag of snails falls to the floor. The snails crawl out of it and all over the place.

Edna opens the door and looks angrily at her husband. She says, "And just where the hell have you been?"

Henry looks down at the snails and says, "I told you guys to walk faster!"

• • •

Why will the meek inherit the earth?

They won't have the balls to refuse it.

• • •

How does a man know when his wife is cheating on him?

He buys a used car and finds her dress in the back seat.

• • •

How do you know when you have too many zits?

A blind man comes along and tries to read your face.

• • •

How does a bulimic girl feed her cat?

She throws up in its dish.

• • •

What do rednecks do on Halloween?

They pump kin.

• • •

A well-dressed man walks into a bar and says to the bartender, "I'd like a glass of sixty-year-old Scotch."

The bartender, figuring the man won't know the difference, pours him a shot of ten-year-old Scotch. The man drinks it and says, "I asked for sixty-year-old Scotch. This is ten-year-old Scotch."

The bartender, still figuring the well-heeled man won't know the difference, pours him a shot of thirty-year-old Scotch. The man drinks it and says, "This is thirty-year-old Scotch. I asked for sixty-year-old Scotch."

By this time, a crowd has gathered around the well-dressed man. No one can believe the man truly knows the difference between new and old Scotch.

The bartender goes down into the cellar and pours the man a shot of rare forty-year-old Scotch. The man drinks it and says, "This is forty-year-old Scotch. Don't try and fool me. I know all about Scotch."

The bartender gives up and pours the fussy customer a shot of the rarest Scotch the bar has to offer. The man drinks it and says, "Now that's sixty-year-old Scotch."

Meanwhile, at the end of the bar, a grizzled old man slides a glass down the bar to the expert. The old man says, "Taste it, and do your best."

The man takes a sip and spits it out. "What the hell is this?" he asks.

"It's my piss," the old geezer says. "Tell me how old I am."

• • •

You know you're a redneck if:

Your father walks you to school because he's in the same grade.

Somebody asks you for ID, and you show them your belt buckle.

You go to family reunions to pick up women.

• • •

Why do wives close their eyes when they make love?

They hate to see their husbands have a good time.

• • •

Hear about the Godfather with Alzheimer's disease?

He'll make you an offer he can't remember.

• • •

A man goes to his doctor. The doctor examines him and says, "I have terrible news. You have AIDS, and you also have Alzheimer's."

The patient breathes a sigh of relief. "That is terrible news," he says, "but at least I don't have AIDS."

• • •

How did Captain Hook meet his death?

He wiped his ass with the wrong hand.

• • •

How did the blind girl's parents punish her?

They left the plunger in the toilet bowl.

• • •

How many New Yorkers does it take to screw in a lightbulb?

None of your fucking business.

• • •

What's brown and sounds like a bell?

Dung.

• • •

What's the definition of ridiculous?

A hooker who sues you for sexual harassment.

• • •

Why did the leper quit working out in the gym?

He threw his back out.

• • •

The husband goes to his physician and says to him, "Doctor, I don't know what to do. I want to make love to my wife, but I can't seem to get her excited."

The doctor hands the husband some pills. "Put one of these in her drink tonight," the doctor instructs. "I guarantee it will work."

That evening, the husband drops one of the pills into his wife's drink. Just for the hell of it, he drops one in his own drink, figuring if it's good for her, it must be good for him. To be on the safe side, he drops two more pills in her drink, then drops two more into his own.

They down their drinks. Five minutes later, his wife jumps up from the table and rips her clothes off. "Lordie," the wife exclaims. "I really feel like having me a man tonight."

The husband says, "That's funny. So do I."

• • •

What goes Hop, hop. Skip, skip. Boom!?

Bosnian children playing in a minefield.

• • •

What do census takers do in Bosnia?

They add up the number of arms and legs and divide by two.

• • •

What do women wear in Bosnia?

Tank tops.

• • •

Did you hear about the Jehovah's Witness with Alzheimer's disease?

He knocks on your door for no reason.

• • •

What's well cooked and comes on a stick?

Joan of Arc.

• • •

How did the blind guy cut his fingers?

He tried to read the cheese grater.

• • •

Did you hear about Bosnia's football team?

They caught a lot of bombs.

NOW THAT'S REALLY SICK!

• • • • • • •

Why is life like a cock?

When it's soft, it's hard to beat; when it's hard, you get screwed.

• • •

What's the best thing about contraceptive sponges?

After sex, women can wash the dishes.

• • •

Jake is eighty years old. Dorothy is also eighty. They are having an affair in the nursing home. He goes into Dorothy's room every day and sits on her bed, where she takes his aging pecker in her hand and just holds it for an hour or so.

They do this for several months, then one day Jake doesn't show up in Dorothy's room. She waits until the next day, but he doesn't show. A week later, she hunts him down and asks him where he's been.

"I miss holding your cock in my hand," she tells him.

Jake confesses, "I've been seeing Mrs. Schwartz in room ten. She holds my cock much better."

Dorothy is furious. She asks Jake, "What has Mrs. Schwartz got that I haven't got?"

Jake responds, "Parkinson's Disease."

What do you call ten feminists in a refrigerator?

Cold cunts.

• • •

"Daddy, Daddy, what's a transvestite?"

"Shut up and unhook my bra!"

• • •

What do you call a virgin who just lost her cherry on a waterbed?

The Red Sea.

• • •

Hear about the new all-female delivery service?

It's called UPMS—they deliver whenever the fuck they feel like it.

• • •

Hear about the lovesick gynecologist?

He looked up an old girlfriend.

• • •

So the old man walks into a whorehouse and says to the madam, "I want to get me laid. I hear tell you got lots of pretty ladies here."

The madam eyes the old man suspiciously and asks him, "Just how old are you, Pop?"

"Ninety-two."

"Ninety-two?" the madam exclaims. "Hell, Pop—you've already had it."

"Well then," the old man asks, reaching into his back pocket for his wallet, "how much do I owe you?"

• • •

What's big and brown and lays in the woods?

Smokey the Hooker.

• • •

What do you get when you cross a Hell's Angel with a Jehovah's Witness?

Someone who knocks on your door early in the morning and tells you to go fuck yourself.

• • •

So the guy goes to the whorehouse. Once in the room with the blond hooker, he puts fifty dollars on the bed and drops his pants.

The hooker gasps—the guy's got an eighteen-inch cock.

She says, "I'm not putting that inside me! I'll lick it, I'll suck it, but that's all."

"Forget it," the guy says, taking back his fifty bucks. "I can do that myself."

• • •

What's the difference between eating sushi and eating pussy?

The rice.

• • •

How do blondes part their hair?

They spread their legs.

• • •

What do you call a dog with three legs?

Tippy.

• • •

What do women and beer bottles have in common?

They're both empty from the neck up.

• • •

What do you get when you turn three blondes upside down?

Three brunettes.

• • •

What's the definition of uptight?

A chick who puts a rubber on her vibrator.

• • •

A woman goes to the family doctor. She says, "Doctor, I have a problem. Every night my husband falls asleep with his erect penis inside me."

"Why is that a problem?" the doctor wants to know.

"The problem is," the woman says, "my husband walks in his sleep."

• • •

Why is beer better than a woman?

A beer doesn't get mad when you grab another.

• • •

Why are hangovers better than women?

Hangovers go away.

• • •

The doctor says to his patient, "Sam, I have bad news. You only have six months to live."

"Oh, my God," Sam says. "That's terrible. What should I do?"

"Go get married," the doctor says. "It'll be the longest six months of your life."

• • •

What do soybeans and dildoes have in common?

They're both meat substitutes.

• • •

Why did God create women?

Because sheep are lousy cooks.

• • •

A girl from Alabama walks into a bank, carrying a bag filled with nickels and dimes.

The bank teller says to her, "Gracious, did you hoard all that money by yourself?"

"No'm," the girl says. "My sister whored half of it."

• • •

What's a nymphomaniac's definition of frustration?

A guy with a fourteen-inch dick and herpes.

• • •

What's better than a cold Bud?

A warm Busch.

• • •

Why do husbands lie to their wives?

Because wives keep asking questions.

• • •

What do you call a woman who can suck an orange through a garden hose?

Darling.

• • •

A man makes love to his wife. Afterward, he complains to her, "How come you never tell me when you're having an orgasm?"

"Because you're never around when I do," the wife says.

• • •

How do you know when your girlfriend is frigid?

You spread her legs, and the light in the refrigerator goes on.

• • •

How can you tell a guy has an older sister?

His eye is shaped like a keyhole.

• • •

A fat woman walks into a department store and says, "I'd like to see a bathing suit in my size."

"So would I," says the clerk.

"What have you got in my size?" the fat woman asks.

"The freight elevator," the clerk replies.

• • •

Where does a female pilot sit?

In a cuntpit.

• • •

Why do women wear skirts?

To hide the No-Pest strip.

• • •

How do you tell if a woman is wearing pantyhose?

If she farts, her ankles will swell.

• • •

How do you tell if a woman is wearing underwear?

Look for the dandruff on her shoes.

• • •

Why do women have vaginas?

So men will talk to them.

• • •

Why do men die before their wives?

Because they want to.

• • •

Why are feminists so strong?

Because they have to support themselves.

• • •

How are a bowling ball and a woman different?

Your fingers don't smell when you stick them in a bowling ball.

• • •

How are a woman and a can of tuna different?

It doesn't take five beers to open a can of tuna.

• • •

Why do women get periods?

Because they deserve it.

• • •

Why are the cunt and asshole so close together?

So you can carry them like a six-pack.

• • •

Why are there ten million abused women in America?

Because they never shut the fuck up!

• • •

What do you call a woman with no arms and legs on a hamburger bun?

Patty.

• • •

What's the difference between a married man and a single guy?

A married man has a better half; a single guy gets lots of pieces.

• • •

What do you call an epileptic in a vegetable garden?

A seizure salad.

• • •

A young man goes to see his shrink and says, "Doc, you just got to help me. Every night I have the same dream: I'm lying in bed and five gorgeous women come in, try to tear my clothes off, and have wild sex with me."

"And what do you do?" the shrink asks.

"I push them away," the young man says.

"And what do you want me to do?" the shrink asks the young man.

"Break my arms!"

• • •

What do you get when you mix orange juice and milk of magnesia?

A Phillips screwdriver.

• • •

What do you call a gay dwarf?

A low blow.

YOU KNOW YOU'RE WHITE TRASH WHEN . . .

Your children have head lice as pets.

Your neighbors spray their phone with Lysol after you use it.

Your parents share the same set of false teeth.

Your IQ and your wife's bra size are the same.

You set your bed on fire when trying to light your farts.

Your sister used to date Lobster Boy.

Your idea of a wet dream is winning a case of Budweiser.

You kiss your grandmother and she slips you the tongue.

You blow your entire welfare check on lottery tickets.

Hear about the Polish employee?

They wanted to pay him what he was worth, but he wouldn't work that cheap.

• • •

Hear about the Polish loser?

His swimming pool burned down.

• • •

How do you know when your marriage is in trouble?

On your wedding night, she says, "I think we're seeing too much of each other."

• • •

How do you know when you're a loser?

You join the KKK and they burn a cross on *your* lawn.

• • •

A man goes to see his physician and says, "Doc, you won't believe this, but every time I sneeze, I have an incredible orgasm. What do you recommend?"

The doctor replies, "Black pepper."

• • •

Here's the bad news: Adolf Hitler is still alive and is living in Argentina.

Here's the good news: He's finally going to be tried for all his crimes against humanity.

Here's worse news: He's being tried in L.A.

• • •

What do you call it when your girlfriend puts ice cream on her twat?

Hair pie à la mode.

• • •

What's the best way to avoid rape?

Beat off your attacker.

• • •

Two young brothers, aged five and six, are listening through the keyhole as their older sister is getting it on with her boyfriend.

They hear her say, "Oh, Jim, you're going where no man has gone before!"

The six-year-old says to his brother, "He must be fucking her up the ass!"

• • •

What's the difference between an Italian woman and a dead dog?

You can eat a dead dog.

• • •

A man goes to a prostitute and hands her the agreed-upon fee of fifty dollars.

Getting undressed, the hooker asks him, "What would you like to do?"

The man replies, "I'd really like to have wild sex and then spank you."

The hooker asks, "How long do you want to spank me?"

The man replies, "As long as it takes to get my fifty dollars back."

• • •

The marriage counselor asked the husband, "Why did you throw apples at your wife when you had your last fight?"

"Because," the husband replied, "watermelons were out of season."

• • •

What's gay and jerks off into washing machines?

The Mayfag repairman.

• • •

What do a priest and a Christmas tree have in common?

They both have balls that are just for decoration.

• • •

It's Joe's turn to have the guys over for poker. Unfortunately, his wife has to work late and he can't find a babysitter for his twelve-year-old son, Joe Junior.

The kid is annoying everyone, walking around the poker table and yelling out which cards the men are holding. Joe and his buddies are getting fed up, because every time Joe chases his son away, the kid comes back and continues yelling out the different hands.

Finally, Joe grabs his son and takes him into the bathroom, then comes back to the table and picks up his cards. Half an hour later, one of the guys remarks, "Hey, Joe—where's your kid? We ain't seen him in a while. What did you do, kill him?"

"Nah," Joe replies. "I taught the kid how to jerk off."

• • •

What's blue and comes in brownies?

Cub scouts.

• • •

Why do mutes masturbate with only one hand?

So they can moan with the other.

• • •

What's the definition of an Indian agent?

Someone who only takes ten percent of your scalp.

• • •

What's the difference between a porcupine and Congress?

Porcupines have their pricks on the outside.

• • •

What is a transvestite's philosophy of life?

Eat, drink, and be Mary.